D0745851

WEST VIRGINIA

by Jonatha A. Brown

GARETH**STEVENS**

Please visit our web site at: www.garethstevens.com
For a free color catalog describing Gareth Stevens Publishing's
list of high-quality books, call 1-800-542-2595 (USA) or
1-800-387-3178 (Canada).

Library of Congress Cataloging-in-Publication Data

Brown, Jonatha A.
    West Virginia / Jonatha A. Brown.
        p. cm. — (Portraits of the states)
    Includes bibliographical references and index.
    ISBN-10: 0-8368-4711-3 — ISBN-13: 978-0-8368-4711-6 (lib. bdg.)
    ISBN-10: 0-8368-4728-8 — ISBN-13: 978-0-8368-4728-4 (softcover)
    1. West Virginia—Juvenile literature. I. Title. II. Series.
    F241.3.B76   2007
    975.4—dc22   2005036643

This edition first published in 2007 by
Gareth Stevens Publishing
A Weekly Reader® Company
1 Reader's Digest Road
Pleasantville, NY 10570-7000 USA

This edition copyright © 2007 by Gareth Stevens, Inc.

Editorial direction: Mark J. Sachner
Project manager: Jonatha A. Brown
Editor: Catherine Gardner
Art direction and design: Tammy West
Picture research: Diane Laska-Swanke
Indexer: Walter Kronenberg
Production: Jessica Morris and Robert Kraus

Picture credits: Cover, pp. 4, 12, 18, 21, 27, 29 © Pat & Chuck Blackley;
p. 5 U.S. Fish & Wildlife Service; p. 6 Steve Shaluta/West Virginia Division of
Tourism; pp. 7, 9, 10 © North Wind Picture Archives; p. 15 © Gibson Stock
Photography; pp. 16, 26, 28 David Fattaleh/West Virginia Division of Tourism;
p. 17 © Steve Powell/Allsport/Getty Images; p. 22 © Roger Ressmeyer/CORBIS;
p. 24 © John Elk III; p. 25 © AP Images

Printed in the United States of America

2 3 4 5 6 7 8 9 11 10 09 08 07

CONTENTS

★ ★

Chapter 1 Introduction........................4

Chapter 2 History.........................6

Time Line.......................13

Chapter 3 People.......................14

Chapter 4 The Land.......................18

Chapter 5 Economy.......................22

Chapter 6 Government.......................24

Chapter 7 Things to See and Do.............26

Glossary.......................30

To Find Out More.................31

Index.......................32

Words that are defined in the Glossary appear
in **bold** the first time they are used in the text.

On the Cover: The town of Harpers Ferry lies among wooded hills.
This pretty town once played a big part in West Virginia's history.

Introduction

If you could visit West Virginia, what would you like to do there? Hike through a quiet green forest in search of a waterfall? Ride down a river in a raft? Go to a lively music festival or a crafts fair? This state is full of fun things to do!

West Virginia has an interesting history, too. It is the only U.S. state that was once part of another state. It also played a big role in the Civil War. Today, people here are proud of their past. They still carry on some of the old ways as they look forward to the future.

West Virginia is a wonderful place. You are sure to love it!

Cold mountain water tumbles over Blackwater Falls in the Monongahela National Forest.

The state flag of West Virginia.

WEST VIRGINIA FACTS

- Became the 35th U.S. State: June 20, 1863
- Population (2005): 1,816,856
- Capital: Charleston
- Biggest Cities: Charleston, Huntington, Parkersburg, Wheeling
- Size: 24,078 square miles (62,362 square kilometers)
- Nickname: The Mountain State
- State Tree: Sugar maple
- State Flower: Rhododendron
- State Animal: Black bear
- State Bird: Cardinal

History

The first people to live in West Virginia were Native Americans. Among these early people were the Adena. They came to this area more than two thousand years ago. They lived in villages and built big mounds of earth. Some of the mounds were used as graves.

In about 1600, other Natives moved to the area. They included people of the Cherokee, Delaware, and Shawnee tribes.

Explorers and Settlers

In 1606, the British claimed this land as part of the Virginia **colony**. Yet no white person visited the area for many years. The first whites arrived in 1669. That year, John Lederer headed west from the Atlantic coast. He went as far as the Blue Ridge Mountains. Two years later, Thomas Batts and Robert Fallam explored farther west. These men crossed the

The Adena people built this big burial mound long ago. Today, you can see the mound in Moundsville.

Allegheny Mountains and reached the New River.

White settlers moved to this area during the 1700s. They found that living on the **frontier** was hard. The mountains made travel slow. The Natives and the settlers fought. The British and the French fought each other, too. All of these groups were fighting over land.

In 1763, the British king tried to ease the problems. He did not allow settlers to live west of the mountains. Still, the number of whites in this area grew. By 1775, more than thirty thousand settlers lived there. Most were farmers.

The State of Virginia

The Revolutionary War was fought from 1775 to 1783. Few battles took place in what is now West Virginia. After this war, the whole area became part of the state of Virginia.

The western part of Virginia was different from the rest of the state. In the western counties, most of the people lived on small

The British explored this area in the 1700s. They cut arrows on trees to mark the borders between colonies.

FACTS

Who Came First?

The first white settler in West Virginia may have been a man from Wales. His name was Morgan Morgan, and he reached the area in 1726. Morgan built a cabin next to Mill Creek. More people settled nearby, and a town grew up along the banks of the creek. Some people say a group of Germans reached West Virginia before Morgan. These people founded the town of New Mecklenburg at about the same time.

IN WEST VIRGINIA'S HISTORY

The Raid at Harpers Ferry

John Brown was a white man who hated slavery. He thought slaves should band together and fight their owners. He wanted to get guns for this fight. In 1859, he and a small group of men attacked a storehouse full of guns at Harpers Ferry. They took over the **armory** for one day. Then, the U.S. Marines arrived and took the armory back. John Brown was hanged for his crime. Even so, he became a hero to people who wanted slavery to end.

the nation. The western part of Virginia was more like the Northern states.

Civil War and a New State

In late 1860, the Southern states began to pull out of the **Union**. They formed a new country. They called it the Confederate States of America. But the North did not want the South to break away. This led to the Civil War in 1861.

farms. Few farmers owned slaves there. Farther east, big farms were common. Slaves did most of the work.

Many farmers in the South kept slaves. On the other hand, most Northern states did not allow slavery. Many people there wanted slavery to be banned all over

Famous People of West Virginia

"Stonewall" Jackson

Born: January 21, 1824, Clarksburg, West Virginia

Died: May 10, 1863, Chancellorsville, Virginia

Thomas Jackson was born in western Virginia. He grew up to be a famous army **general**. When the Civil War began, he fought on the side of the South. At the First Battle of Bull Run, many Southern soldiers ran away. Jackson's fighters did not run. One watcher said they stood "like a stone wall" to fight the Northern troops. Jackson went on to win many battles. He died after being shot by mistake by one of his own men.

Soon after the war began, Virginia joined the Confederacy. Most people who lived in the western counties were against this change. These counties broke away from the rest of the state. They formed a new state that was known as Kanawha. A few weeks later, they changed its name to West Virginia. In 1863, West Virginia became a U.S. state. Most of its people fought for the North in the Civil War.

FUN FACTS

What's in a Name?

The city of Charles Town was founded in 1788. It was named after George Washington's brother Charles. The name was later changed to Charleston.

9

Dozens of battles were fought in the new state. Farms, bridges, and whole towns were destroyed.

In 1865, the Union won the war. Now the people of West Virginia had to rebuild their damaged state. They built railroads and factories. Coal mining towns sprang up along the railroad tracks.

Trouble for Coal Miners

Mining soon provided jobs for thousands of men. They worked long hours in unsafe places. Mines sometimes caved in, killing the men inside. In 1907, hundreds of men died in an explosion at a mine in Monongah. It was the worst mining **disaster** in U.S. history.

In 1912, miners in Paint Creek and Cabin Creek held **strikes**. They refused to go back to work until the mine owners agreed to make the workday nine hours long. Fighting broke out, and more than twenty people were killed. Others were sent to jail. Even so, the workers did not go back to

Coal miners pose in front of a mine in the early 1900s. Work in the mines was very hard and the pay was low.

FUN FACTS

Changing Capitals

When West Virginia became a state, its first capital was Wheeling. The capital was moved to Charleston in 1870. Then, it was moved back to Wheeling. In 1885, it was moved to Charleston again. This city has been the state capital ever since.

IN WEST VIRGINIA'S HISTORY

Help from the U.S. Government

In the 1950s, people who lived in the mountains of West Virginia were some of the poorest people in the country. Many men could not find jobs. President John F. Kennedy wanted to help. In the early 1960s, he set up programs to help bring business to the state. The programs also provided money for job training and health care. They helped many poor people have better lives.

work for more than one year. Finally, the mine owners agreed to their demands.

Strikes and even **riots** continued for years. In 1921, striking miners in Mingo County fought against police and the U.S. Army for four days. After these men were beaten, most other miners did not dare to fight for their rights. In the 1930s, a new law helped the miners. This law allowed them to band together and bargain with mine owners.

In the 1950s, coal miners faced a different problem. Machines took over their jobs. Many men were out of work. Thousands of miners left the state to find jobs.

The State Today

These days, coal mining still provides jobs in West Virginia. Although mines are safer now, accidents still happen. In 2006, sixteen miners died in four separate mining accidents. Labor **unions** continue to work with mine owners to make mines safer.

Mining has left piles of waste and patches of bare land. Factories have also caused problems. They have dumped poisons into the air and water. The people of West Virginia are trying to fix these problems and restore the land to its natural beauty.

Today, West Virginia's streams are much cleaner than they were thirty years ago. State laws now protect both land and water.

IN WEST VIRGINIA'S HISTORY

Flood!

In 1972, a dam on Buffalo Creek burst. It had been holding back a huge amount of water and coal waste. A wall of water 20 feet (6 meters) high raced through the valley. The flood killed more than one hundred people. After this, **strict** laws were passed. Today, mining companies must clean up waste and fix land that has been scarred by mining.

★ ★ ★ Time Line ★ ★ ★

about 1000 B.C.	The Adena people live in what is now West Virginia.
1600	Other Native tribes reach the area.
1669	John Lederer becomes the first white man to see West Virginia.
1726	Morgan Morgan builds a cabin on Mill Creek and becomes one of the first white settlers in this region.
1775	More than thirty thousand whites live in the western part of the Virginia colony.
1775–1783	The Revolutionary War is fought.
1859	John Brown and a group of men raid the armory at Harpers Ferry.
1861–1865	The North and South fight the Civil War.
1863	West Virginia becomes a U.S. state and fights for the North in the Civil War.
1912	Coal miners go on strike. They refuse to work until mine owners agree to shorter working hours.
1972	A dam on Buffalo Creek breaks. The flood that follows kills more than one hundred people.
1977	A law is passed to force mining companies to clean up the land they have used for mining.
2006	Sixteen miners die in four separate mining accidents.

People

The people of West Virginia are known as Mountaineers. Their name comes from the state's nickname, which is The Mountain State. The first white settlers in this rugged land were often poor, but they were strong and willing to work hard. Today, Mountaineers are proud of their background. Many are as strong and hardworking as the early pioneers.

In most U.S. states, more people live in the cities than in the country. Yet, West Virginia is different. Almost two-thirds of

Hispanics

This chart shows the different racial backgrounds of people in West Virginia. In the 2000 U.S. Census, 0.7 percent of the people in West Virginia called themselves Latino or Hispanic. Most of them or their relatives came from places where Spanish is spoken. Hispanics do not appear on this chart because they may come from any racial background.

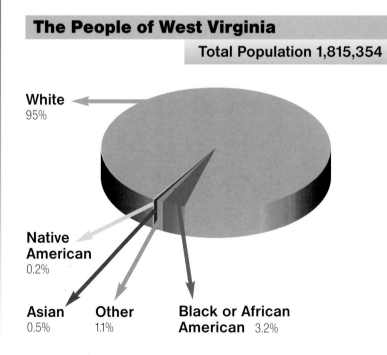

The People of West Virginia

Total Population 1,815,354

White
95%

Native American
0.2%

Asian
0.5%

Other
1.1%

Black or African American 3.2%

Percentages are based on the 2000 Census.

the people here live in the country. They live in small settlements or on farms. Only about one person in three lives in a large town or a city. In all, fewer than two million people live in the state.

The Kanawha River flows through the city of Charleston. Charleston is the state capital and the largest city in the state. About fifty-three thousand people live here.

The People of the Past

Most of the white settlers in this region were from Britain and Ireland. Thousands of people came from Germany, too. Most of these settlers built small farms.

After the Civil War, people came to the state to work in the mines and on the railroads. Some worked in lumbering. They came from Hungary, Poland, and Russia. African Americans also moved to West Virginia. They came from the states farther south.

15

The People Today

Today, few people move to West Virginia from other parts of the world. Most of the people who live in this state were born in the United States.

About 95 percent of the people in West Virginia are white. African Americans make up 3 percent of the **population**. The rest are Asian, Native people, or a mix of races.

Religion

As in the rest of the country, most people in West Virginia are Christian. Many of these people are Methodists and Baptists. This state also has Roman Catholic and Protestant churches.

Education

Before West Virginia became a state, most parents paid fees to send their children to private schools. Some church groups ran schools, too. Those schools were free. Classes were often held in log cabins that also served as churches.

In 1863, the new state set up a public school system. It provided only for grade

Fans turn out for a football game at West Virginia University. More than twenty-six thousand students attend this school. It is the biggest university in the state.

Mary Lou Retton won more medals at the 1984 Summer Olympics than any other athlete.

schools at first. After 1908, the state supported public high schools as well.

The first college was founded in 1837. This was Marshall University in Huntington. Today, Marshall is still serving students. The state has many other colleges and universities, too. The largest one is West Virginia University in Morgantown.

Famous People of West Virginia

Mary Lou Retton

Born: January 24, 1968, Fairmont, West Virginia

As a little girl, Mary Lou Retton loved gymnastics. She started taking lessons when she was seven years old. When she was fourteen, she moved to Texas so she could work with a top-ranked coach. She went to the Olympic Games in 1984. Retton wowed the crowd there. She became the first American to win the individual all-around gold medal! She also won two silver and two bronze medals at the games. She became one of the most famous Olympic athletes of her day.

The Land

West Virginia is called the Mountain State for good reason. It is a land of rugged mountains and steep hills. There is little flat land here.

Ridges, Valleys, and a Plateau

West Virginia lies in the Appalachian Mountains. The state is made up of two natural regions. The Ridge and Valley Province covers the eastern part of the state. This area deserves its name. It is filled with narrow ridges and steep valleys.

The Allegheny **Plateau** lies to the west. It covers more than two-thirds of the state. In ancient times, the land here was high and nearly flat. Later, rivers and streams cut through the ground. They

The Appalachian Mountains run through the eastern edge of the state.

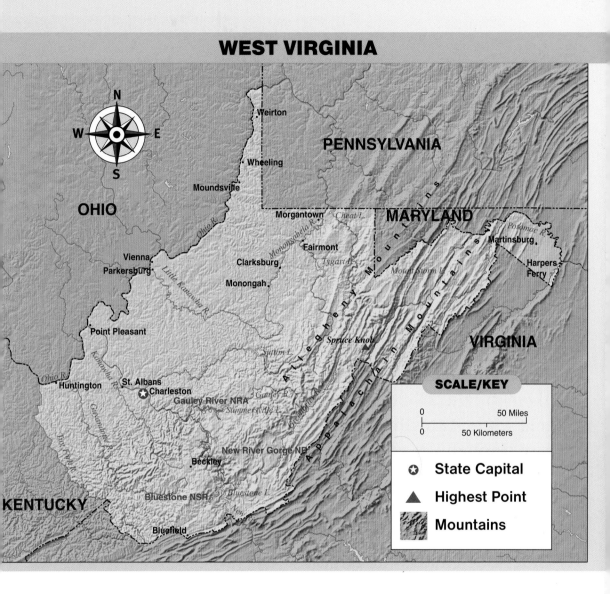

Map labels: Weirton, PENNSYLVANIA, Wheeling, Moundsville, OHIO, Morgantown, Cheat L., MARYLAND, Potomac R., Monongahela R., Fairmont, Martinsburg, Vienna, Clarksburg, Tygart L., Mount Storm L., Harpers Ferry, Parkersburg, Little Kanawha R., Monongah, VIRGINIA, Ohio R., Point Pleasant, Sutton L., Spruce Knob, Kanawha R., Ohio R., Huntington, St. Albans, Charleston, Gauley River NRA, Gauley R., Summersville L., New River Gorge NR, Greenbrier R., Beckley, Twelvepole R., Bluestone NSR, Bluestone L., KENTUCKY, New R., Bluefield, Allegheny Mountains, Appalachian Mountains

SCALE/KEY

0   50 Miles

0   50 Kilometers

⊛ State Capital

▲ Highest Point

▨ Mountains

created the hills and valleys that now crisscross most of West Virginia.

The highest point in the state is in the plateau. This peak is Spruce Knob. It is 4,861 feet (1,481 m) high.

Waterways

The state of West Virginia has an odd shape and wiggly borders. Some of its borders are formed by rivers. The northwestern border is made by the Ohio River. West

19

Virginia lies on one side and the state of Ohio lies on the other side.

The Tug Fork River crosses the land farther south. It forms the border between West Virginia and Kentucky. In the northeast, the Potomac River divides the state from Maryland.

Many rivers run through West Virginia. The largest of them are the Monongahela and Little Kanawha. They run through the plateau and drain into the Ohio River.

Some rivers have been dammed to create big lakes. Bluestone Lake is the largest of the man-made lakes in the state. It was formed when a dam was built on the New River. West Virginia has no big natural lakes.

Climate

In West Virginia, summers are warm and winters are

Major Rivers

Ohio River
975 miles (1,569 km) long

Potomac River
287 miles (462 km) long

Little Kanawha River
160 miles (255 km) long

cool to cold. The higher parts of the state are cooler than the lower parts. The whole state gets plenty of rain, and thunderstorms sometimes cause major floods in low areas.

Plants and Animals

West Virginia is a very green state. Trees cover about three-fourths of the land. The sugar maple is the state tree. Pine, beech, oak, and many other kinds of trees also grow here. In the spring, cherry, dogwood, and redbud trees bloom.

Many kinds of animals make their homes in West Virginia. Black bears prowl in the woods. Deer, skunks, foxes, and bobcats can be seen, too. Mink and otters live near the waterways.

This state is home to many different types of birds. The cardinal is the state bird. It is very common. Hawks, eagles, woodpeckers, and ducks are just a few of the other birds that can be seen here. Many different kinds of snakes and fish live in West Virginia, too.

FUN FACTS

The Old New River

West Virginia is a state with many natural wonders! One of the greatest is the New River. Despite its name, this is one of the oldest rivers in North America. The New River flows through canyons that are more than 1,300 feet (396 m) deep. Some parts of this beautiful river flow slowly. Other parts have rapids. Each year, thousands of people visit the river. Some come to enjoy its beauty. Others test their skill at whitewater rafting.

The beautiful New River is not new at all. In fact, it is thought to be one of the oldest rivers in the world!

Economy

West Virginia is one of the nation's top coal-producing states. When coal prices are high, the state does well. When prices fall, many people are out of work. The state also has good supplies of natural gas and oil. Sand, salt, and clay are mined here, too.

Farms and Forests

About twenty thousand farms are in this state. Because the land is hilly, most farms are small. The top farm products are beef cattle, hay, and chickens. Other products are turkeys, pigs, apples, corn, and oats.

Forestry also provides jobs in this state. Forestry workers harvest trees and saw them into lumber.

Coal mines provide jobs for many people in West Virginia. These men are working about 800 feet (244 m) underground in a mine near Wana.

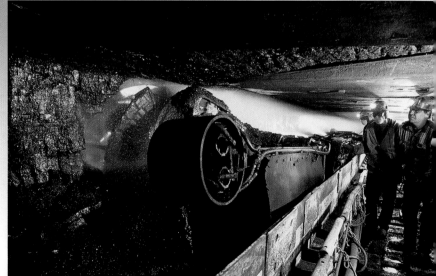

Glass, Car Parts, and More

About one in nine workers in West Virginia have factory jobs. Some of these workers use the natural gas and sand in the state to make glass. First, they heat furnaces with gas. Then, they melt sand in the furnaces. This melted sand turns into glass.

Other factories produce car parts, wood and plastic products, and clothing. Clay from the Ohio River is used to make pottery.

Tourism

Large numbers of tourists visit this state each year. Many of these people come to fish and hunt. Tourists eat in restaurants, sleep in hotels, and spend money in stores. These places need workers. In all, about fifty thousand people in the state have jobs in tourism.

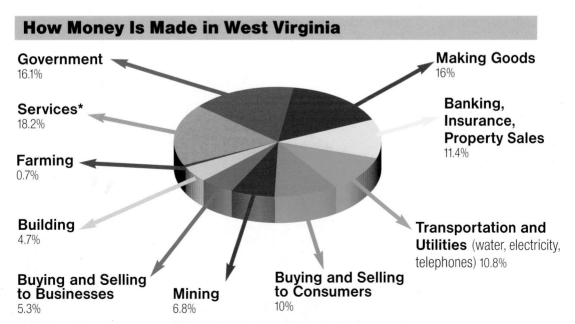

How Money Is Made in West Virginia

Government 16.1%

Services* 18.2%

Farming 0.7%

Building 4.7%

Buying and Selling to Businesses 5.3%

Mining 6.8%

Buying and Selling to Consumers 10%

Making Goods 16%

Banking, Insurance, Property Sales 11.4%

Transportation and Utilities (water, electricity, telephones) 10.8%

* Services include jobs in hotels, restaurants, auto repair, medicine, teaching, and entertainment.

Government

Charleston is the capital of West Virginia. The state's leaders work there. The government of the state has three parts. These parts are the executive, legislative, and judicial branches.

Executive Branch

The executive branch carries out the state's laws. The governor is the leader of this branch. A group of people known as the **cabinet** help the governor.

The state capitol building is in Charleston. The beautiful dome on top is covered with gold.

These West Virginia state senators are holding a meeting in the state capitol in 2005. State legislators meet several times each year. Most of their meetings are held between January and early April.

Legislative Branch

The legislative branch makes laws for the state. It has two parts. They are the Senate and the House of Delegates. These parts work together to make the laws.

Judicial Branch

Judges and courts make up the judicial branch. They may decide whether people who have been **accused of** committing crimes are guilty.

Local Governments

West Virginia has fifty-five counties. Each county is run by a county court. Three people serve on each court. Most of the towns and cities in the state are led by a mayor and council.

WEST VIRGINIA'S STATE GOVERNMENT

Executive		Legislative		Judicial	
Office	Length of Term	Body	Length of Term	Court	Length of Term
Governor	4 years	Senate (34 members)	4 years	Supreme Court of Appeals (5 justices)	12 years
Secretary of State	4 years	House of Delegates (100 members)	2 years	Circuit Court (65 judges)	8 years

Things to See and Do

West Virginia is a great place to learn about the past! You might like to start at the West Virginia State Farm Museum in Point Pleasant. There you can visit a one-room schoolhouse and two old log cabins. You can also see old farm tools, railroad cars, and much more. Both Wheeling and Charleston have good museums, too. These museums also focus on state history.

A coal miner shows visitors through the exhibition mine in Beckley.

Beckley is home to an exhibition coal mine. You can ride through the mine on mining cars. The guides are real coal miners. They will take you through mine shafts and explain how coal was mined in the old days.

Making Music and Crafts

If you like **bluegrass** or country music, you are sure to love this state. You can hear toe-tapping tunes at festivals all year long. In fact, no event here seems

West Virginia is known for its fine trout and bass fishing. Here, two fishermen try their luck on the Greenbrier River.

Famous People of West Virginia

Francis H. Pierpont

Born: January 25, 1814, near Morgantown, West Virginia

Died: March 24, 1899, Pittsburgh, Pennsylvania

Francis Pierpont is known as the Father of West Virginia. In 1861, he did not want the state of Virginia to leave the Union. Even so, Virginia broke away and joined the Confederacy. Pierpont thought this was wrong. He knew that many people in the western counties felt as he did. He helped them break away from Virginia. With Pierpont as their leader, they formed a new state. It became West Virginia. The new state joined the Union in 1863.

to be complete without a few fiddles, **mandolins**, and **dulcimers**. If you're in the mood, get up and dance! Few people can sit still after the fiddlin' begins!

West Virginia is known for handmade crafts, too. You can see lovely quilts, pottery, and baskets at fairs and shops all over the state. If you visit in June, do not miss the Mountain Heritage Arts and Crafts Festival. This three-day event takes place near Harpers Ferry.

Bluegrass musicians put on a show at an outdoor festival. Festivals like this are held all over the state in the summer.

Almost no one stays dry on a whitewater rafting trip! This crew is getting soaked as they shoot the rapids on the famous Gauley River.

Famous People of West Virginia

Anna Jarvis

Born: May 1, 1864, Webster, West Virginia

Died: November 24, 1948, West Chester, Pennsylvania

Anna Jarvis came from a family of eleven children. She was very proud of her mother. She wanted to have a special day set aside to honor all mothers. Jarvis worked hard to convince government leaders to create this special day. In 1915, her dream came true. President Woodrow Wilson announced that the second Sunday in May would be known as Mother's Day.

The Great Outdoors

West Virginia is full of natural beauty. Each year, thousands of people come to this state to enjoy the rivers and mountains. Some hike or ride horses or mountain bikes in the Monongahela National Forest. Many head down the rivers in canoes, kayaks, and rafts. One of the most exciting rivers is the Gauley River. It was the site of the 2001 World Rafting Championships.

GLOSSARY

accused of — blamed for

armory — a building where guns are stored

bluegrass — a lively kind of country-style music that uses guitars, fiddles, and other stringed instruments

cabinet — a team of people who help a leader

colony — a group of people living in a new land but keeping ties to the place they came from

disaster — bad accident

dulcimers — musical instruments with three or four strings that are strummed or plucked

elevation — height

frontier — a place that is being settled by pioneers

general — a high-ranking officer in the armed forces

mandolins — musical instruments like lutes that have four to six pairs of strings

plateau — a large, flat area that is higher than the land around it

population — the number of people who live in a place, such as a state

riots — wild, violent acts by angry crowds

strict — firm, exact

strikes — work stoppages caused by workers who are trying to get better pay or working conditions

Union — the United States of America

unions — groups that try to get better pay and working conditions for workers in factories, mines, or other businesses

Books

Appalachia: The Voices of Sleeping Birds. Cynthia Rylant (Voyager Books)

In Coal Country. Judith Hendershot (Dragonfly Books)

M Is for Mountain State: A West Virginia Alphabet. Discover America State by State (series). Mary Ann McCabe (Sleeping Bear Press)

West Virginia. This Land Is Your Land (series). Ann Heinrichs (Compass Point Books)

West Virginia Facts and Symbols. The States and Their Symbols (series). Kathy Feeney (Capstone)

Web Sites

Enchanted Learning: West Virginia
www.enchantedlearning.com/usa/states/westvirginia/

West Virginia Coal Mining Facts
www.wvminesafety.org/wvcoalfacts.htm

West Virginia Kids' Page
www.legis.state.wv.us/Educational/Kids_Page/kids.html

West Virginia State Farm Museum
www.wvfarmmuseum.org

Adena people 6, 13
African Americans 14, 16
Allegheny Mountains 7
Allegheny Plateau 18–19
Appalachian Mountains 18
Asian Americans 14

Batts, Thomas 6
Beckley 26, 27
Blackwater Falls 4
bluegrass music 27–28
Blue Ridge Mountains 6
Bluestone Lake 20
Brown, John 8, 13
Buffalo Creek 12, 13

Cabin Creek 10
Charleston 5, 9, 11, 15, 24, 26
Cherokee people 6
Civil War, U.S. 8–10, 13, 15
climate 20
coal 10, 11, 13, 22, 26, 27
counties 11, 25
country music 27–28

education 16–17

Fairmont 17
Fallam, Robert 6
farming 8, 10, 15, 22

Gauley River 29
Germany 8, 15
Great Britain 6, 7, 15

Harpers Ferry 8, 13, 28
Hispanics 14
Huntington 5, 17

Jackson, "Stonewall" 9
Jarvis, Anna 29

Kanawha 9
Kanawha River 15
Kennedy, John F. 11

labor strikes 10–11
lakes 20
Lederer, John 6, 13
Little Kanawha River 20

Mingo County 11
mining 10–12, 13, 15, 22, 26, 27
Monongah 10
Monongahela National Forest 4, 29
Monongahela River 21
Morgantown 17, 28
Mountaineers 14
mountains 18
music 27–28

Native Americans 6, 7, 13, 14
New Mecklenburg 8

New River 7, 20, 21

Ohio River 19, 23
Olympic Games 17

Paint Creek 10
Pierpont, Francis H. 28
Point Pleasant 26
Potomac River 20

rafting 21, 29
railroads 10, 15
religion 16
Retton, Mary Lou 17
Revolutionary War 7, 13
Ridge and Valley Province 18
rivers 19–20

Shawnee people 6
slavery 8
Spruce Knob 19

tourism 21, 23
Tug Fork River 20

Virginia 6–9, 13, 28

Wana 22
Washington, Charles 9
Washington, George 9
West Virginia University 16, 17
Wheeling 11, 26
whitewater rafting 21, 29
Wilson, Woodrow 29